Pennies

By Mary Hill

SCHOLASTIC INC.

New York Toronto London Auckland Sydney
Mexico City New Delhi Hong Kong Buenos Aires

Thanks to T Bumble's Toys in Swarthmore, PA

Photo Credits: Cover © Ken Cavanagh/Photo Researchers, Inc.; pp. 5, 7 © Royalty-Free/Corbis; p. 9 © Inc, MedioImages/Index Stock Imagery, Inc.; p. 11 © Lester Lefkowitz/Corbis; p. 13 © James L. Amos/Corbis; p. 15 © Charles O'Rear/Corbis; pp. 17, 19, 21 by Maura B. McConnell
Contributing Editor: Shira Laskin
Book Design: Mindy Liu

ISBN 0-516-24891-X

12 11 10 9 8 7 6 5 4 3 2   5 6 7 8 9 10/0

Printed in the U.S.A.   61

First Scholastic printing, February 2005

Contents

These are **pennies**.

Pennies are made of **copper** and **zinc**.

5

Abraham Lincoln is on the front of the penny.

He was the sixteenth president of the United States of America.

The **Lincoln Memorial** building is on the back of the penny.

9

The Lincoln Memorial is a **statue** in Washington, D.C.

It was built to **honor** Abraham Lincoln.

Pennies are made by the **United States Mint.**

The United States Mint is a part of the **government.**

13

The United States Mint makes a lot of pennies every year.

A penny is worth one cent.

It takes one hundred pennies to make a **dollar**.

Many people save their pennies.

Some people put their pennies in a **bank**.

If you save your pennies,
you can buy many things.

New Words

bank (**bangk**) a place where people save their money or a small object in which people save coins

copper (**kop**-ur) a reddish-brown metal

dollar (**dahl**-uhr) an amount of money equal to one hundred pennies

government (**guhv**-urn-muhnt) the people who control a country or state

honor (**on**-ur) to give praise or an award

Lincoln Memorial (**ling**-kin muh-**mor**-ee-uhl) a statue in Washington, D.C., that was made to remember Abraham Lincoln

pennies (**pen**-eez) small metal coins that are reddish-brown in color, and are each worth one cent

statue (**stach**-oo) a sculpture of a person or animal that is often made of stone, metal, wood, or clay

United States Mint (yoo-**nite**-ed **states mint**) a part of the government under the Department of Treasury that makes and gives out money in the United States

zinc (**zingk**) a blue-white metal

To Find Out More

Book
The Coin Counting Book
by Rozanne Lanczak Williams
Charlesbridge Publishing

Web Site
The Adventures of Penny
http://www.kidsbank.com/the_story/penny/index.asp
Learn about pennies and other types of money on this
informative Web site.

Index

About the Author
Mary Hill is a children's book author. She has written books about many different subjects.

Reading Consultants

Kris Flynn, Coordinator, Small School District Literacy, The San Diego County Office of Education

Shelly Forys, Certified Reading Recovery Specialist, W.J. Zahnow Elementary School, Waterloo, IL

Paulette Mansell, Certified Reading Recovery Specialist, and Early Literacy Consultant, TX